August 2014

Second Edition

DEDICATION

To my family,
Linda, Kimberly and Gregory:
Your support and love keep me going.
I'm spoiled, I know it, and I love it.
Love you all.

ACKNOWLEDGEMENTS

Without the critiques from Linda and Kimberly,
I couldn't have written this labor of love.

ACKNOWLEDGEMENTS

To my friend Morris Gresham
who started all of this for me.
He showed me how to get started
and along this journey
his encouragement, critiques and gentle pushes
were priceless in getting me here.

Senior Readers Theatre
Scripts and Skits

Table of Contents

Up or Down

By

Rodney Nall

Cast:
Margaret and Ed: Married couple
Ed, "Mr. Wonderful", in his opinion.
Location:
It's the home of Margaret and Ed.
As Margaret enters, it's obvious she's upset with Ed.

Margaret – Ed you did it! You did it again!!
You didn't put the toilet seat down and I just fell in!

Ed – (Laughing)

Margaret – Laugh all you want, but by tomorrow morning,
my, you know, my backside is going to be black and blue!
(Ed is laughing so hard he can hardly speak)
Stop it, what's so funny anyway?

Ed – I'm sorry honey, it just strikes me as funny that you are
so worried about you're ah, backside being black and blue.
(He can't stop laughing) I just was wondering who was going
to see it? (More laughter)

Margaret – The seat stays DOWN, DOWN, DOWN!

Ed – Just a minute Margaret, whose responsibility
is it to make sure that the seat is always down?

Margaret – It's the man's responsibility. Everyone knows
that. It's a law, I-I-I-I think; I think it was even voted on.

Ed – That's nonsense, and if anyone voted on it,
it had to be those women libbers or whatever.

Margaret – Well, if it was brought to a vote, I know who
would win.

Ed – So, you're saying if it was voted on, the women would win. Is that what you're saying? Well, that can be settled for once and all, right now. All in favor that it's the man's responsibility to put the seat down, hold up your hand. See Margaret, no one voted with you.

Margaret – Well surprise, surprise! We're the only two people here.

Ed – That's right, and that means I won!

Margaret – I've never heard so much hog wash in all my born days. I'd love to hear you explain that.

Ed – Okay, who's the biggest?

Margaret – Well, that's easy. You're a whole lot bigger than me, but what has that got to do with the price of tea in China anyway?

ED – Just be patient with me, will you? Who's the oldest?

Margaret – You are. Come on, Ed.

Ed – Who's the tallest?

Margaret – You are.

Ed – So there, it's so obvious, that my vote should have more weight. Therefore, I win!

Margaret – That doesn't prove a thing.

Ed - Who uses the bathroom more, me or you?

Margaret – I do but-t-t-t....

Ed – Who gets up most during the night?

Margaret – I do.

Ed – So, it makes more sense that you put the seat down.
You need to check it every time.
It's not my responsibility!
It's the same as if it was a user fee.
It should be according to usage.
I rest my case.

Margaret – Don't you try to spin your way out of this when you know that I KNOW THAT I AM RIGHT. YOU'RE JUST TRYING TO CONFUSE ME.

Ed – Doesn't the seat lift up and down?

Margaret – Well, yes it does.

Ed – The seat is not heavy. You can lift it, can't you?

Margaret – Come on now, you've got to do better than that to even convince yourself, much less me.

Ed – Alright Margaret, this is what really happens. Sometimes you tell me to put the seat down and sometimes that I should put it up. I just get so-o-o confused. Up or down, down or up. It's like knowing what to do about daylight savings time. I get so confused. Is it fall back and spring forward or is it, fall forward and spring back? I never know. You must realize that I am only a man. Sometimes I forget things.

Margaret – You only forget what you want to.

Ed – Margaret, you know how it is with guys. First you start to forget names and then you forget faces. Then you forget to pull up your zipper,   but it's worst when you forget to pull your zipper down.

Margaret – O.K. Ed, I give up. You win. I've tried for thirty years to change you and I should know better than to keep trying. If I didn't love you, I'd just put a knot on your head and say forget it. I suppose I'll just have to keep you as you are.

Ed - Margaret, I love you too and I will try to do better. You will have to agree that nobody does a better job carrying out the trash or drying the dishes.

Margaret – Now Ed, we're getting pretty mushy and sentimental. Let's go watch The Lawrence Welk reruns. That will certainly bring back some good memories.

TV Doctor & Cleanliness

By

Rodney Nall

Ed - I can't believe I was able to pull you away from Dr. Fred's TV Show. I'm starving and I hear this restaurant has good food.

Margaret - Dr. Fred was a rerun from yesterday. Did I tell you what yesterday's discussion was about?

Ed - Yes you did, twice, and I'll never forget, I promise.

Margaret - You just can't learn too much from Dr. Fred. This restaurant is new, but just look at how dirty the glass doors are. Let me see your handkerchief, I just can't stand these dirty doors.

Ed - Forget it Margaret, we're blocking the door.
This place is busy, where do you want to set?

Margaret - Just anywhere, I don't care.

Ed - This booth looks good.

Margaret - You know I don't like booths, I'd like a table.

Ed - Here's a table. This one will do just fine.

Margaret - You better get your glasses changed, this table is filthy.

Ed - Where's the filth? It looks like water spots to me.

Margaret - How do you know what it is? It could be anything. Dr. Fred says.......

Ed - OK Margaret, I'll call the waitress and have her clean it up.

Margaret - You'll do no such thing. No telling how awful our service will be if you start complaining.

Ed - Fine, let's sit at the table in the corner.

Margaret - Why do you have to be so difficult? We'll never get service stuck way back there.
Besides that, the door to the kitchen is next to the table and I hate all that traffic. Then there's all those smells coming from the kitchen and... Let's just sit here.

Ed - Good, "THEN SIT DOWN!

Margaret - Well, you don't have to be so testy.
People are staring at us. They can see how difficult you are. Besides that, we can't sit down yet.

Ed - What, are you nuts? If you think that I'm going to eat standing up.......

Margaret - Edward, I'm just thinking of your well being. You get more like your daddy every day. I remember when.......

Ed - Okay Margaret, Okay, I'm beyond being embarrassed. What now?

Margaret - Just hold my satchel while I look through it.

Ed - What are you doing? You are being ridiculous, people are pointing at us and whispering.

Margaret – Never mind them, just be still. I have a roll of toilet paper and a can of Clorox spray cleaner in my satchel.

Ed - You're killing me. Here's your precious spray.

Margaret – No, no, no! I need the Clorox Cleaner. Have you ever read the label on this product? Of course you haven't. It says that this product will kill on contact. The Clorox Spray is in my bag? It's in the yellow can.

Ed - Is this what you're looking for?

Margaret – That's it. Just look how good it sprays.
That ought to kill anything.

Ed – Okay, okay, okay! Just start cleaning.

Margaret – Ed, would you just be patient? Your mother warned me how impatient you can get. This is straight from Dr. Fred's book on good hygiene. Spray, wipe dry, spray again and wipe dry. Dr. Fred says that will kill 99% of all germs.

Ed - Okay, I've learned more than I ever wanted to know and I could probably pass a test on hygiene. Sit down. We're blocking the aisle.

Margaret - You always have to have your way, don't you Edward? I just try to take care of your health and do you appreciate it? No! I haven't cleaned the seats yet. You never know who has been sitting here. My Aunt Lizzy, bless her soul. You remember my Aunt Lizzy? Of course you do. Well, Aunt Lizzy caught a ... well you remember what she caught from a toilet seat so you can never be too careful. Dr. Fred says to go on the side of caution. Dr. Fred says, it's better to be safe, than sorry.

Ed – Hurry up and spray the darn seats! (Ed starts to have a coughing fit). Whoa, stop it. That stuff is too strong. My eyes are running (coughing).....My eyes are burning. Put it away. How much does it take anyway?

Margaret - The label says a little goes a long way, but Dr. Fred says...

Ed - I know, I know. Dr. Fred says to err on the side of caution, but you're going to kill us both with cleanliness.

Margaret - You'll thank me when you don't have to go to the Dr. next time.

 Ed - What are you talking about?
 How will I know that I didn't have to go to the doctor if I didn't have to go?

Margaret - Just get another roll of toilet paper out of my satchel so I can dry off the chairs.

Ed – Now, can we sit down? My knees are killing me?

Margaret - Did you take your pain medication this morning? No, of course you didn't!
You know the medicine doesn't work if you leave it in the container, don't you? It's just like your hearing aid, which you refuse to wear. If I've told you once, I've told you a thousand times….

Ed - Just pick up your menu and order.

Margaret - Is your menu dirty? Just look at mine, It looks as if someone dribbled beef stew all over the back of it.

Ed - Here, take mine. It's clean.

Margaret - Well, Dr Fred says, when you touch anything that's not sterile, wash your hands with hypo-allergenic soap.

Ed - Okay, clean your hands and let's place our order.

Margaret – Well, you've got the wipes. They're in my satchel on your side of the table.

Ed - Okay Margaret, I'll clean my hands and you clean yours. Then let's order.

Margaret - Okay Ed, I'm happy now. The table top and the chair seats are all sanitized. The menus are clean and here comes the waitress. Get out your Senior Discount Card. This place gives 10 percent off after four pm. I'm so hungry I may even order dessert.

Ed - Margaret, do you have my wallet? It's not in my jacket pocket. I distinctly remember putting it in my pocket before we left the house.

Margaret - Oh yeah! I needed a couple of ones, so I just got a twenty and a couple of fives. I guess I laid the wallet down when the phone rang. It's not my fault you don't have it. You should always check your pockets before you leave the house? Dr. Fred says there's a place for everything and everything should be in its place.

Ed - Just what has that got to do with you and my.....oh, never mind? We have no money. We have to go home.

Margaret - There are a couple of TV dinners in the freezer and some left over iced tea.

Ed – I guess we can eat those and watch the Ed Sullivan reruns.

Margaret - Here's a sanitized wipe. Be sure you use it after you touch the doorknob.
Dr Fred says ...

A Mighty Fine Meal"

By

Rodney Nall

Cast:
Ed, the loving husband, has a way with words.
Margaret, the loving wife,
has a few words of her own.
Location:
Both are relaxing in the family room after dinner.

Ed – Yes sir that was a mighty fine meal Margaret. Yes sir, that was mighty fine.

Margaret – Well, thank you Ed. You haven't complimented me on a meal in years. I really appreciate it.

Ed – Yes sir, that meal was something to write home about.

Margaret – Just stop it Ed! You're going to make me cry, and you know when I start crying, I can't stop.

Ed – Well, don't start sobbing yet. It's just been so long since I had a real tasty, home cooked meal, I just thought you'd like to know.

Margaret –   Ed Blakely, you take that back. You know as well as I do that I cook for you every day of the year.

Ed – You haven't done any real cooking in years. Not since you got that gosh awful microwave. You throw something in it and two minutes later, bingo, hot rubber chicken or meatloaf so tough that you can bounce it. You call that cooking?

Margaret – Now, I am really upset. If it's been so bad all these years, how come you kept cleaning out your plate, every meal, for over thirty years?

Ed – I never had a choice. I can't cook, and every- thing in the fridge is frozen. Besides, I've been supplementing my meals with peanut butter for years, and we always have plenty of Pepto-Bismol. Yes sir that was a mighty fine meal. It reminds me of the meals that my mother used to cook.

Margaret – Your mother never knew a casserole from a pot roast. Everything she cooked was fried, burnt or covered with white gravy. It was always fried potatoes, fried okra, fried squash, fried chicken, fried tomatoes and the worst of the lot, fried bananas!
No wonder you used to drink so much sweet tea.

Ed – Well, like it or not, fried food is good for you. It kills all the germs. You have to chew it, and that's good for your teeth. Being raised in the south, if it wasn't burnt, it wasn't done. Besides that, my mama did so cook something besides fried food.

Margaret – If that's so, just name one thing.

Ed – I sure can. Just about every week we had a pot of pinto beans. We would eat on them all week, and they sure weren't fried! Just take that miss smarty, and put it in your microwave!

Margaret – How could I have forgotten those gosh awful pinto beans? I'll grant you that. They sure weren't fried.
They floated in so much salt pork and fat back for seasoning that they might as well have been a fried food. You were so spoiled that you hardly ever ate a vegetable.

Ed – That's a lie and you know it.

Margaret – It is not!

Ed – Is too!

Margaret – I've got you this time.

Ed – I'll show you missy prissy. How about mustard?

Margaret – Oh, you did eat a lot of mustard, to cover up the taste. Besides that, mustard is not a vegetable.

Ed – Is too!

Margaret – Is not, is not, is not!

Ed – Well, it sure ain't an animal or mineral, miss smarty pants.

Margaret – Your hopeless, stubborn, pig headed, and, and, I don't know what else.

Ed – Well, I can tell you another vegetable, "CATSUP"!!!!!!!

Margaret – Catsup, catsup, are you crazy?
Catsup comes in a bottle and is full of sugar.
Besides that, tomatoes are a fruit!

Ed – Are not!

Margaret – Are too!

Ed – What's catsup made of? It's red, ripe tomatoes, fresh from the bottle. You can't tell me that's not a vegetable. I've seen tomatoes growing on the vine. Vegetables grow in a vegetable patch and fruit grows in an orchard.

Margaret – I give up. There's no reasoning with you.

Ed – (loud burp) Oh, excuse me. That just slipped out.

Margaret – It sometimes happens to all of us after a good meal.

Ed – What were we talking about? I seem to have forgotten. Let me see.

Margaret – Oh, I remember, you were telling me just how much you enjoyed your meal and how good it was.

Ed – Mighty good meal, yes sir, a mighty good meal ZZZZZZZZZ!

Margaret – Ed, are you dozing off?
Yes sir that was a mighty good meal!

Because I said so!

By

Rodney Nall

Cast:
Margaret has a full time job taking care of Ed.
Ed has his own view of how things should be.
Location:
Margaret is preparing the morning meal for Ed.

Margaret - Edward, your breakfast is on the table. Finish what you are doing and get in here while it's hot.

Edward- I'm really hungry. While you've been cooking I've been watching the morning news and snacking. Did you know how good popcorn tastes when you find it unexpectedly?

Margaret- Just where did you find any popcorn? I've already vacuumed up what you dropped last night. It's supposed to go in your mouth, not on the floor!

Edward- I found the popcorn between the seat cushions. It tasted real good.

Margaret- I found popcorn all over the floor in front of your recliner. If I've told you once, I've told you a thousand times, slow down your eating, so it goes into your mouth, not on the floor!

Edward- I can't stand to eat it kernel by kernel like you. I like to eat it by the handful. That's probably the reason it fell on the floor. You're lucky you have a good vacuum cleaner. Where's my breakfast?

Margaret- It's right in front of you. You're looking at it.

Edward- What is that stuff?

Margaret- It's your breakfast!

Edward- Seriously, what's that?

Margaret- It's scrambled eggs!

Edward- I've never seen scrambled eggs that

looked like that. They're white. I want real yellow eggs.

Margaret- It's scrambled egg whites.
I'VE NEVER SEEN ANYONE SO PECULIAR!

Edward - What are you doing?

Margaret - You want color, I'll giving you color.

Edward - What are you pouring on my eggs?

Margaret - It's yellow food coloring. You want yellow? You got yellow!   Now stir them up and eat.

Edward - What are you trying to do to my breakfast?

Margaret - It's what your doctor ordered. Egg whites, toast, with no butter, soy sausage, and decaf coffee.

Edward - I want real eggs, real bacon, real coffee and who eats dry toast?

Margaret - Your doctor said…..

Edward - Yeah right, but the doctor doesn't have to eat it.

Margaret - I work so hard trying to take care of you and you just love to scream at me.

Edward - Where did you put the salt shaker?

Margaret - Taste your food first. Then, if you need salt, I'll get the shaker for you.

Edward – You know I always salt my food before I touch it.
That's the way I've always done it.
That's the way my mama did it and her mama too!
Why should I change now?

Margaret - You eat entirely too much salt so I've hidden the shaker. If you really need more after tasting your food, I'll go get it.

Edward - Get the shaker. I'm going to need it.

Margaret- Your cholesterol and blood pressure are too high.
You are overweight and too much sodium is bad for you.
TRY IT FIRST!!

Edward - If my mother was here she wouldn't make me do
without salt. What have you done with the strawberry preserves?
I can't eat breakfast without strawberry preserves on my toast and
I need real coffee!

Margaret - You have to watch your sugar, and caffeine raises
your blood pressure. Just eat your breakfast. You don't
appreciate the sacrifices I make for you.

Edward - Okay Margaret, if you are willing to sacrifice for me
then it's the least that I can do to.................
Wait just a second, what's that on your plate?

Margaret - Don't be silly; it's just a couple of scrambled eggs, five
pieces of bacon, buttered toast, strawberry preserves, and a large
cup of my favorite coffee.

Edward - WHAT?

Margaret - It's simple. You have your doctor and I have mine.
My doctor says at my age, I can eat what I want!

ED – Good-bye Margaret!

Margaret - Edward where are you going? It's not like you to leave
food on your plate.

Edward - I'll just wait for lunch to eat.
Comparing my breakfast to yours, I lost my appetite.

Margaret - Well, I've got news for you. Your lunch isn't going to
be any better.

Ed - What are you saying?

Margaret - Your doctor says to stick with soy food. You're
having spaghetti sauce made with tofu and soy crumbles served

over whole wheat spaghetti. I know you don't like it but get use to it!

Edward - Margaret, how about signing me up with your new doctor? He sounds like my kind of man.

Margaret - He is a she, and I'm sorry about that Edward, but you had your chance when I signed up. Now, she's not taking any more new patients.

Edward - I may get healthier but I'll probably starve getting there.

Eating Out

By

Rodney Nall

Cast:

Margaret and her loving husband Ed..

Location:

Margaret and Ed, at home, discussing where to eat out.

Scene 1

It's Saturday Night and Ed is taking Margaret out to eat

Margaret - Ed, it's time you started getting ready. We need to leave soon. It's already seven o'clock.

Ed - What do you mean get ready? I am ready!

Margaret -   You've got to be kidding. We'll never get in the front door of any restaurant, the way you look. You look terrible. They might let us eat in the kitchen. Go put on some clean clothes we'll never get good service with you dressed like that?

Ed- What are you talking about? I put these clothes on fresh just two days ago.

Margaret- Those clothes are filthy. You've been mowing the yard all day in those clothes. Look, your shirt has food stains from breakfast and whatever that is, I really don't want to know.

Ed - Listen Margaret, I've already washed those breakfast stains out with a wash cloth. I shook the grass clippings out of my pants, and I'm ready to go.

Margaret - You're not going with me, looking like that! You need a shave and shower! Ed Blakely, get upstairs and take a shower NOW while I lay out your clothes.

Ed - Margaret, I'm not a baby.

Margaret - Well, you act like one. Don't forget to use a washcloth, soap, water, and that new herbal shampoo I ordered from the TV shopping program. It smells strong enough that it should cover up anything you miss.

Ed - I shaved last Saturday and this is only Wednesday.

Margaret - Ed Blakely, you are cleaning up. It's bad enough the way you look around the house, but I'm taking you out in public. Put on clean underwear and clean socks, too. Hurry up, I'm starving.

Ed - My word Margaret, you'd think that we were going to the Ritz-Carlton or something. The older you get, the more peculiar you become.

Scene 2

Margaret and Ed are finally on the way to the restaurant

Margaret - I worked all day while you were just messing around. I haven't been off my feet all day. I did three loads of laundry, ran the dish washer, cleaned two bathrooms, vacuumed and put fresh linens on the bed. I even took a bubble bath so I'd smell good for you.

Ed - Okay, Ok I hear you. Where do you want to go to eat?

Margaret - I don't care. You decide.

Ed - I decided last time. As a matter of fact, I've had to decide every time.

Margaret - Ed, I know how peculiar you are. Just say where you want to go. It makes me no difference.

Ed – Okay, let's eat barbecue!

Margaret - NO! Not barbeque. I can't eat that
spicy stuff this late at night. Anything else is fine,
just name it, I don't care.

Ed - I've thought of the perfect place, Mexican food at El
Fritos.

Margaret – It's El Pablo's, and I can't eat there.
If I have Mexican food too often, I have reflux or whatever.
Ed, if you weren't so difficult, we could find a restaurant.

Ed - Okay, I just thought of the perfect place, Willie's Beer
Palace! They have hotdogs, fries, onion rings, half price beer
for seniors, and mud wrestling every weekend.

Margaret - I remember that place and no, we are not eating
there again. Their hotdogs are terrible!

Ed - What are you talking about? Your mother loved
Willie's.

Margaret - My mother just agreed to go so you wouldn't
whine all night.

Ed - That woman could really put away the beer and when it
came to food, I'll never forget them cutting out all you can
eat night, just because of your mother. Okay Margaret, it's
getting late, where do you want to go eat?

Margaret - As I said thirty minutes ago EDWARD,
just pick a place. You know I'm not the picky one in our
family.

Ed - Margaret you are driving me crazy. Let's try the Green
Frog. We can't go wrong with their blue plate special.

Margaret - Okay, but you know that's not my favorite spot and I'm not eating their blue plate special. It's always liver and onions or sauerkraut and wieners.

Ed - How much money do you have on you? The Green Frog only takes cash. I spent all my money.
I bought oil for the mower, a bag of fertilizer and I forgot to go to the bank before it closed.

Margaret - Why didn't you tell me sooner? I have over thirty dollars hidden in the fridge in an old coffee can for emergencies.
Now it's too late to go home, get the money and get to the restaurant before it closes. Wait a minute! Look here, I just remembered that I have some rolled coins in my purse.

Ed - If you think I'm going to pay our bill with rolled coins, you've got another think coming. I'd be so embarrassed. Why, those people would think that I don't have any cash.

Margaret - Well DUH, you don't have any cash.
You spent what you had, didn't go to the bank and you didn't let me know. We are going to the Green Frog. We're not ordering the blue plate special, and you are paying the bill with my coins. I'm tired and hungry. Let's just go there, NOW!

Ed - Okay, Okay, settle down Margaret. With my great sense of direction, we'll be at the Green Frog in just a few minutes.

Margaret - That's just fine with me EDWARD, but we are going the wrong direction. Turn around. Go back to Center Street. Take a right, then left on fifth, and we're there.

Ed - Okay, okay, okay. Would you like to listen to the radio? It just might soothe your nerves?

Margaret - NO! You only listen to country music and I need something like classical music. Never mind, we're almost to the restaurant.

Ed - See, I knew where I was going.

Scene 3
The meal is just about over and…………………..

Margaret - Ed, I have never been so embarrassed in all my life. First, you screamed about how high the prices were. Then, your food wasn't hot enough. Next, you complained to the waiter about dirty silverware.

Ed - Margaret, you know how I am about dirty dishes. I just wanted clean silverware.

Margaret - Your fork was dirty, but the only reason it was dirty was because it was your salad fork. You had already used it. The way you carried on, we're lucky they didn't kick us out.

Ed - When I have to pay these prices, I expect everything to be perfect. This place has an attitude. They probably won't even give us our senior citizen discount.

Margaret - One look at you and they'll know you are a senior citizen.

Ed - You know how I love salad, and I couldn't get a refill. They cut me off after four iced tea refills, and you know what? They'll probably expect a tip, but that will be a cold day in….

Margaret -That's enough Ed. You're talking so loud that people are staring at us. The salad was what you ordered. You could have ordered a large one, but NO, to save money, you choose the child's portion. I was embarrassed the way you kept swigging the tea and running back and forth to the bath room. You ARE leaving a tip!

Ed - Look at this ticket. It looks as if they charged us for everything. I'm surprised they didn't charge us for using this table. Margaret, what's seven percent of $11.50?

Margaret - What's that? Where did you come up with seven percent?

Ed - Isn't that the sales tax rate? You have to base your tip on something.

Margaret - I really need to take you out in public more often. The tip is based on what your bill is.

Ed - O.K. Margaret, but these people can retire on the tip I have to leave. How much is $11.50 times ten percent?

Margaret - You're only leaving ten percent? Nobody gives ten percent any more.

Ed - What's wrong with ten percent?

Margaret – First, it increased to fifteen and now it's up to twenty percent. If you can't figure it out, let me.

Ed - That's crazy. Just who decided to raise tips?
Who decided that? Since seven percent is good enough for the government and ten percent is good enough for the churches, it ought to be good enough for the restaurants.

Margaret - You old tight wad, you're just trying to embarrass me.

Ed - Okay Margaret, have it your way, but I may have to get a part time job just to pay our tip money.

Margaret - You poor thing. Just count out twenty-three dimes.

Ed - Twenty-three dimes? I should change my name to Rockefeller. Here Margaret, do something with all these Coin wrappers.

Margaret - What have you done? You unrolled all the coins. Now, I'll have to count out dimes, nickels and pennies just to pay our bill.

Ed - If you didn't want me to unroll all those coins, why did You give them to me?.

Margaret - I had a senior moment and forgot who I was dealing with. My mother told me before we married that you were a tight wad. She said one evening you offered her a piece of gum and told her that it cost a nickel. When she offered to pay for it, you took it. Let's pay our bill and get out of here.

Scene 4

Margaret and Ed on the way home

Ed - Margaret, would you like some ice cream?

Margaret - I need some to settle my stomach.

Ed - Where would you like to go?

Margaret - I don't care. You decide.

Ed - I chose last time. It's your turn.

Margaret - Just pick a place, I don't care.

Ed - Okay let's go to Barney's Ice Cream.

Margaret - You know that I don't like their selection.

Ed - Margaret, you always pick vanilla.

Margaret - I know, but I like to look at all the flavors.

Ed - Okay, where do you want to go?

Margaret - You know I'm not particular. You pick. Ed, what are you doing? This is our driveway. I thought you wanted ice cream.

Ed - We spent so much time arguing that I lost my appetite and we argued so long, that every place has closed for the night.

Margaret - It's just as well. You don't need the calories. Oh Ed, tomorrow's Sunday. Would you pick up a dozen donuts in the morning for breakfast?

Ed - Sure, what kind do you want?

Margaret - I don't care, you decide. You know I'm not the picky one in the family!

Prescription Medicine

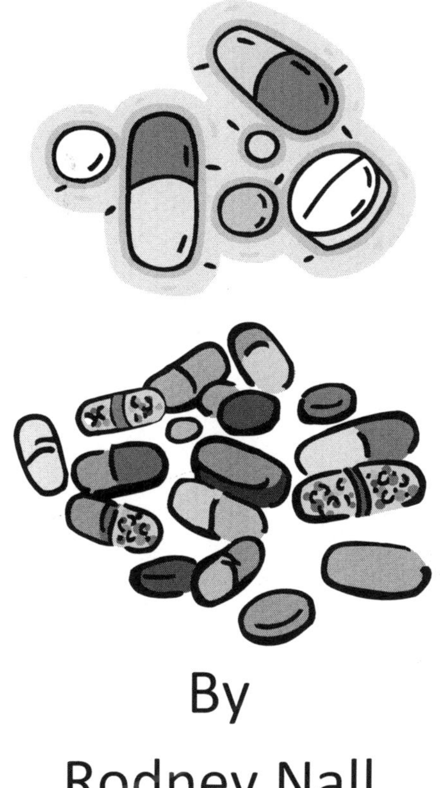

By

Rodney Nall

Cast:

Margaret: The loving wife of Ed has her work cut out for her.
Ed: It's not that Ed doesn't try; it's just that ……

Location:

Home of long time married couple, Margaret & Ed.
A typical day unfolds
as Margaret and Ed go about their daily life.

Ed - MARGARET, Help, Help! Where are you when I need you?

Margaret - What's the emergency? I was cleaning YOUR bathroom, and I have never seen such a mess in all my life. If someone saw that bathroom, they would think that you're growing science projects for the grandkids!

 Ed - What's the matter with the bathroom?
The toilet flushes just fine and the drains aren't stopped up.

Margaret - Never mind, you never notice anything anyway. I need to sit down. I'm out of breath from running all the way to the kitchen. What's the emergency?

Ed - It's not an emergency. I just wanted to ask you a question.

Margaret - Ed, I ran all the way from the other end of the house because you were yelling HELP, HELP, HELP. I was down on my hands and knees, cleaning YOUR toilet when you started screaming for me.

Ed - If you heard me yelling, why did it take you so long to get here?

Margaret - Ed, with my arthritis, you know it takes me forever and a day to get up when I'm on my knees. I came as fast as I could.

Ed - Yeah, I'm sorry but I spilled my seven day pill container. They went all over the floor. I had to sweep them up and I don't know where all the pills go. I think I might have mixed them up.

I found this red pill and I don't remember a red one. They all look so much alike, I guess it doesn't matter where they go.

Margaret - Have you lost your mind---AGAIN? It does matter. You have several blood pressure pills, a cholesterol pill, a water pill, an aspirin, a Claritin, COQ10, fish oil, vitamin pill, vitamin D, iron pill, a garlic tablet, red yeast rice and I'll have to look at the list to see what the rest are.

We don't have any medicine or supplements that are red. Where did you find that funny looking red pill?

ED - It was right here under the table leg.

It looks important! I knew it wasn't mine, so

I put it in your pill box.

Margaret - Ed, no one can take that pill.

We don't even know what it's for.

I order all your pills by mail and I don't remember any red ones. Wait a minute--- you took the dog to the vet. What kind of pills did you get?

Ed - By golly, you might be right. The vet did give me some "worm pills" for the dog. I forgot all about them.

Margaret

And you put that pill in with mine.

You HAVE lost your mind this time.

Ed - You are right. It is the worm pill. They are red.

I'm glad you didn't take it, although it might have cleaned you out real good. I tried to put my pills back, but they all look alike.

Margaret - What are you doing?
Let me see that pill box.
These are my pills you spilled, not yours.
See my name is on the bottom of the box.
None of our medicines are remotely similar.
My blood pressure pills are stronger than yours.
Your cholesterol pills are stronger than mine.
You're supposed to take your own medicines, not mine.
Medications are one thing that we ARE NOT going to share. I've got to get these straightened out. You didn't take any of mine did you?

Ed - I don't think so.

Margaret - You either did or you didn't.

Ed - Well you see, I don't think I took all my blood pressure pills yesterday. That's why I got confused and picked up yours by mistake.

Margaret - ED, you need to take all your medications every day. IS THAT UNDERSTOOD?

ED - It's no problem. I was just going to double up
to make up for what I missed yesterday.

Margaret - You can't do that. How often do you mess up taking your medications?

Ed - Last week, I counted my colon cleansing pills,
for our 21 Day Cleansing Program.
I discovered that I had twice as many AM pills as PM pills, so
I've been doubling up on my AM pills to catch up. Maybe that's
the reason I've been spending so much time in the bathroom.

Margaret - Ed, you've got to use your head.

You never double up on any medications. They provide you just the right amount at just the right time.

Ed - I wish that you would make up your mind.
Last month you were fussing at me about how much our medications cost.
You told me to stop wasting them.

Margaret - That's because I'm always finding pills on the floor (under your chair).
You are always dropping them
when you're getting them out of their bottles.
That's why I got us both pill boxes.
They're more convenient.
We only have to fill them once a week and they're
 ready when needed.
I guess that I was wrong to buy the pill boxes.
Now, instead of dropping a few pills,
you're spilling the entire container.

Ed – Well, it's the manufacturer's fault. It's got that childproof lid, like my medications come in. Just look, the lid on the pill box won't open.

Margaret - Edward, you are trying to open the wrong side. It's no wonder that you spilled them.
See that arrow on the other side. It points to the words, "OPEN HERE".

Ed - Would you look at that? I never noticed that before. The container needs to come with better directions.

Margaret - When did you start reading directions?
In the forty-seven years we've been married, I've never known you to read instructions or directions that come with anything.
Why would you start now?

Ed – Well, it's never too late to start.

Margaret - Ed, I have an idea.

Ed - What do you have in mind?

Margaret - From now on let's fill our pill boxes at the same time.

Ed - Margaret, you're so smart, but you were about to say…

Margaret - We should take our medications together at the same time.

Ed - Margaret, you are a genius. I must also be one for marrying you.

Margaret - While I sort out this pill mix-up, would you get us a couple of glasses of water?

Ed - Water, why do we want water? Are you thirsty? It's not time to eat.

Margaret - So we can take our pills.

Ed - You take your pills with water?
No wonder I have such a hard time swallowing mine.

The Solution

By

Rodney Nall

Ed - Margaret, what brand name is our luggage?

Margaret - It's called "Blockbuster". Why do you need to know that?

Ed - That stuff holds up real good and it lasts forever.

Margaret - That's what the ad says. We've had ours for twenty years. Why?

Ed - I'm going to order me a briefcase, made out of that same stuff.

Margaret - A brief case, why do you need a brief case?

Ed - To carry my stuff in!

Margaret - Your stuff? What stuff?

Ed - I've got a lot of stuff! Stuff that I might need when I'm out and about, or when I'm working in the yard, or out with Moody and Jim at the VFW.

Margaret - What a great idea! There's just one problem. You'd lose it the first day.

Ed - Come on Margaret. Give me a little credit. I've got that covered: Handcuffs!

Margaret - You what? Handcuffs! What are you talking about? My head is beginning to spin.

Ed - You know, like the CIA uses to carry secret documents. You see it all the time in the movies.

Margaret - You are going to lug a briefcase around with you all day long? All day, with it handcuffed to your wrist, to carry your stuff in? Wow, for a minute I thought that you had lost your mind, now I know it!

Ed - Ingenious, isn't it? Everything would be right at my fingertips. Never lose anything. A place for everything and everything in its place!

Margaret - You mean that every time you mow the yard, cut the shrubs, or hoe the garden, you have that ever ready brief case attached to your wrist. You'd probably lose the key the first day and then you couldn't open it.

Ed - That's where you're wrong, I'm getting one with a combination lock.

Margaret - A combination lock?
You can't remember the four letter pin number for our checking account. How can you remember a combination lock number?

Ed - I knew that you'd say that, and I've got it all figured out. I'm going to have the numbers tattooed on my forearm in Chinese. Those Chinese tattoos are really cool.
No one would know what it means, except me.

Margaret - Do you speak Chinese?

Ed - No, why?

Margaret - You would have to read it to remember it.
How are you going to do that if you can't read Chinese in the first place?

Ed - I hadn't thought of that. I'm just trying to get organized.

Margaret - You're seventy years old. Why start now?

ED - Because I'm always losing the grocery list, my loose change, rebate forms and sales receipts.

Margaret - Edward, you need to come up with another idea. Why not do what I do, just stick it in your bra?

Ed - Very funny, I come to you with a really serious problem and what do you do? You make fun of me.

Margaret - Come on now," Mr. Touchy", who drives me crazy every waking moment. Alright, I will get serious.
You need to carry a purse.

Ed - Ha, ha, ha, that's very funny. If you don't want to
Help me, just say so.

Margaret - I am serious. It's becoming the hip thing to do.

Ed - Hip for whom? Not me. I could never do that.

Margaret - Why not? Kiefer Sutherland carries one every week?

ED - Who?
Margaret - I should have known that would be a problem for you, try Jack Bauer.

Ed - Jack Bauer on "24"! He's my favorite actor and "24" is my favorite show. Who's Kiefer Sutherland?

Margaret - He plays Jack Bauer. Don't you ever read the TV Guide?

Ed - I thought his name was Jack Bauer! Besides that, it's not a purse. It's a satchel.

Margaret - Satchel, patchal, what difference does it make? It's better than a brief case handcuffed to your wrist.

Ed – It's okay for a super hero, but for a regular stud like me, it's a little girly looking and the guys would drive me crazy laughing about it . A satchel is a woman thing. After all, I do have a reputation to maintain.

Margaret - Maintain a what? Who are you trying to impress?

Ed - Well, just for your information, when you're not with me at the Senior Center, I catch a lot of women's eyes!
They especially like my hat and my cowboy boots.

Margaret - Just where did you get those silly ideas?

Ed - I haven't told you before, because I didn't want to make you feel bad. They say things like,
"I bet your wife is jealous of your hat".
When I wear my cowboy boots and my gym shorts, I notice them cutting their eyes at me and even whispering to other ladies about me. Now, doesn't that make you jealous?

Margaret - Edward, I hate to break it to you, but I don't think those are compliments.

Ed - How about this? When I leave my shirt unbuttoned to show my hairy chest and abs, a few of the ladies certainly notice, I can tell you that for sure.

Margaret - Just how do you know?

Ed - Basic Biology 101, the body drives some of the ladies so crazy that they suggest I button up. Now what does that tell you, miss jealous wife?

Margaret - It tells me that you are pathetic. I'm going shopping. Have you seen my fanny bag?

Ed - Margaret, you just said the magic word,

"fanny bag". I know what I need.

Margaret - You are going to wear a fanny bag?
Ever since I got mine, all you've done is tell me how fat it
makes me look.

Ed - No, not a fanny bag! Whatever gave you that idea? It
simply gave me my answer; a money belt!
That should hold what I need. I'll never lose anything
again. Thank you Margaret!

Margaret - Well, I'm so glad I can be helpful, but you'll just
have to struggle through life until the stores open
after the holidays. Then you can get it on sale. You know
we never pay full price for anything, anymore.

Ed - That's Okay Margaret, I've found a temporary
solution. In the meantime, I'm going down to the VFW to
test it. See you later.

Margaret - I wonder what that man has come up with. It's
probably better that I don't know. Now where did my new
bra go? I had just taken it out of the package. Oh he
wouldn't, he didn't!
Edward where are you?
Edward, come back here.
EDWARD!!!

Ed Leaves Stage Holding Margaret's New Bra

Roll Back the Clock

Or

Full Speed Ahead

By

Rodney Nall

Cast:
Margaret never knows which Ed will get out of bed.
Ed seems to have a mid life crisis or is just difficult.
Location:
Its home with this Margaret and Ed.
It all started when Margaret said that Ed needed a haircut.

Ed – Nag, nag, nag. Margaret you're driving me crazy. If you don't stop complaining every time   my hair starts curling over my collar, I'm going to let it grow to the floor.

Margaret – No, you're not. I'll put my foot down to that. I will not live with a hippie. You never take a bath and heaven knows that your once a week shower already cuts it pretty close.

Ed – That's it Margaret. You know I shower almost every day and I get stronger every day that I let my hair grow, like Sampson, in the Bible. Sometimes I don't even know my own strength!

Margaret – You know that's pretty funny. You complain about carrying a bag of trash out or when you have to push the vacuum. They're too heavy or it hurts your back or….

Ed – Ok Margaret, you've gone too far. I'm letting my hair grow out, down to the floor. You are about to see a super senior or maybe I'll be called "The Bionic Senior".

Margaret – Grow up Ed! Act your age. You know you're just blowing smoke.

SIX MONTHS LATER,
LET'S JOIN MARGARET AND ED IN THE KITCHEN.
ED"S HAIR HAS GROWN ALMOST TO HIS WAIST.

Margaret – Ed, your breakfast is ready. Hurry up before it gets cold.

Ed – What did you fix me this time?

Margaret - Ed Blakeley, don't start again. You know perfectly well what you're having; Eight ounces of warm prune juice that will …

Ed – Alright!! Alright!! You don't have to tell me what it does. I hate that stuff and I don't need a gallon every morning. Last time you even left the pits in and I almost choked to death. I nearly broke one of my teeth and….
Why don't you buy it at the store like everybody else in America does? Why squeeze your own? This is so thick, I can't drink it. I have to spoon it down.

Margaret – Well Ed, the doctor said a little pulp in your juice is good for you. Besides that, I use the skin and what's left over to make your favorite prune surprise casserole with beets and cabbage and a little cinnamon.

Ed – You know I hate that….what's it called, prune surprise? I always find a surprise in it. Sometimes I believe you clean out the refrigerator and underneath the stove and throw it all in the pot. It's like buying a box of Cracker Jacks and looking for the prize that's always in the box. With yours, it's hard to tell if it's a prize or punishment.

 "OH MY GOLLY, LOOK AT THAT".   It's a long grey hair in my prune juice. It's even wrapped around the spoon.

Margaret – Well, act indignant all you want. Just look in the mirror and you will see where that grey hair in your juice came from. I've had it. I've begged you to get something done to your hair, but you refuse and it has grown almost to your waist. You use almost a bottle of my best shampoo every time you shower. You always use two towels and I –I – I – insist you do something about your hair. It's embarrassing. You already dress like a bum, but the hair, **PLEEEASE!**

ED MAKES AN APPOINTMENT WITH THE BEAUTY SHOP. HE RETURNS HOME THREE HOURS LATER AND JUST TAKE A LOOK AT THE "NEW" ED.

Ed – Margaret, I'm home. I've had my hair done and it does make me look younger. I should have listened to you a long time ago. You know our life, sometimes gets a little boring and I decided you need a new me!

Margaret – Heaven help us! What is that? PLATINUM BLONDE! What have you done?   Are you crazy? My goodness Ed, we have to go out in public every once in a while. What will we do when we go to the VFW monthly bingo, Tuesday morning prayer meeting, breakfast buffet and Saturday morning tour of the neighbor's garage sales? What have you got to say for yourself?

Ed – "Blondes have more fun".

 Come on Margaret, don't get so bent out of shape. Frank Johnson got a convertible. Ed Smith got a trophy wife. Les Moore has two girlfriends. Besides, this makes me feel like a new man, a younger man, a …

Margaret – A divorced man. Ed Blakeley, I won't have it.

Ed – Come on now, Margaret, gimme' a big ole' kiss.

Margaret – Stop it! Get away from me! I feel like I'm kissing a woman. How much did that mess cost you?

Ed – Well, I got it on sale. Today's price was $75.00, but the third time is free. You always want me to save money. I was bargain shopping.

Margaret – I'm so mad I could spit nails. Get that hair cut and get rid of that blonde color if you want anymore meals in this house. ALSO, YOU'LL BE SLEEPING DOWNSTAIRS ON THE COUCH IF YOU DON'T FIX YOUR HAIR!

ED RETUNS TO THE BARBER/BEAUTY SHOP AND RETURNS HOME TWO HOURS LATER WITH HIS HAIR CUT, BUT……

Ed – I hope you're happy. You take away the one pleasure a man has in his life. I hope you're satisfied.

Margaret – What have you done this time?

Ed – Don't worry. I got it cut and had the blonde color removed. In fact, the beautician told me she was sure you'd send me back, so she only used a blonde rinse that could be washed out.

Margaret – Thank goodness for small miracles, but what has she done to you?
That looks like a "RAG MOP"

Ed – I told the lady, that I wanted to look like a teenager or a young adult. I've never seen a beautician drink on the job before. When I walked in the door again, she grabbed a bottle out of her cabinet, Jack Daniels Bourbon, I think, and chug-a-lugged two swigs. It must be a stressful job inhaling all those fumes all day long…..

Margaret –That looks like A RAT'S NEST! You've gone from Moses to Marilyn Monroe to hair like a rock star. I hope I'll be forgiven for what I might do. If I wanted a teeny bopper as a husband, I'd….. Ed, you're hopeless. What will it take for you to

grow up and stop driving me crazy? ANYTHING, just name it.
I'm losing my mind.

Ed – There might be something.

Margaret – Just name it.

Ed – No more home squeezed prune juice and I want real coffee, in fact two cups, AND EGGS, TWO EGGS, FRIED AND BACON, LOTS OF BACON!

Margaret – Ok Ed, you win. Once a month you can have your choice for breakfast and I will start buying regular prune juice. You can have decaf coffee and oatmeal for the other days, deal?

Ed – "DEAL"

LATER ED RETURNS, "THE NORMAL ED"

Ed – Margaret, look.

Margaret – Oh Ed, you're beautiful. My old Ed has come home.

THEIR LOVE LASTS….WELL FOR A WHILE ANYWAY!

Pizza

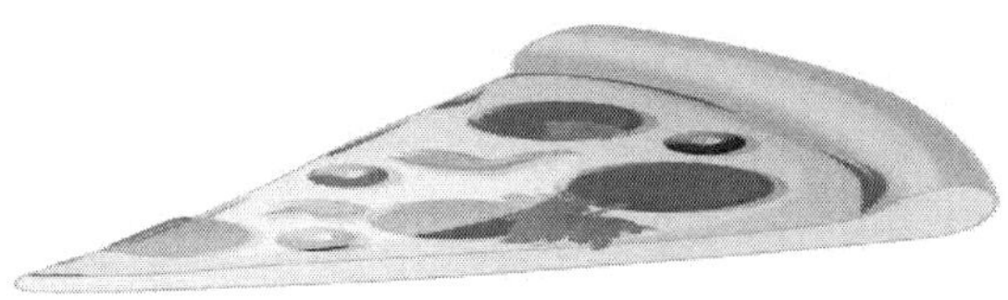

By

Rodney Nall

Ed - Margaret, tonight's Friday night and you know what that means.

Margaret - I can read you like a book. Why don't you just come out and say it? You want pizza. Our Friday nights are just like any other night except you have to have your pizza. I love the pepperoni, sausage and the cheese, but I cannot stand it when you order anchovies. It overwhelms all the other flavors. How can you stand them?

Ed - Okay. Margaret, have it your way. As long as we get the three pizza deal, I'm happy. Rob's Pizza features that pan size, extra thick, extra cheese with extra sauce. He puts so much cheese on his pizzas that you have to use both hands to hold one piece. I love it, but I will miss my anchovies. They give the pizza that little extra.

Margaret - Little extra! You have got to be kidding. When you order "take out" pizza I can smell you coming two blocks away. Last time we had pizza, you promised that we would have "normal" pizza. What did you do? You had the pizza guy cover up all the anchovies with a layer of cheese and jalapenos. You thought I'd never notice. What is it with you and fish anyway?

Ed - You are always preaching to me that I should eat healthy and what is healthier than fish? You made me quit bringing home sardines and you know how I love 'Sardines and crackers.

Margaret - I just couldn't stand the aroma. The garbage man reported us to the health department. He thought you were killing varmints and throwing them in the trash. Your garbage cans were being raided every night by all the alley cats in the neighborhood.

 Ed - It's a shame that people don't mind their own business. They could learn a lot about fine food. I probably should write an article for the local paper. It probably would go national.

Margaret - You fuss at me when I simply slice an onion or squeeze garlic with a garlic press. You tell me that it makes you cry and your eyes burn. You have never thrown away any of your pizza boxes. You act like they are collectables or something. That stale cheese, anchovies smell and stale sauce are becoming a health hazard. Last count, there were one hundred and twelve empty pizza boxes in our garage.

 Ed - Now Margaret, I'm simply doing what you do with all your old yogurt containers. You never know when there might be a contest to see who can collect the most pizza boxes. I'll have a jump start on that contest. I'll cleanup on that deal.

Margaret - Have you ever heard of such a ridiculous contest?

Ed - No, but you know I do have a head for marketing.

Margaret - In your own mind, you do.

Ed - Well I've got an even better idea. The UPC's on the pizza boxes can be very valuable.

 Margaret - Ed, you have got to be a little further up the food chain to even think of that. Carry out pizza doesn't have UPC'S. Just admit that you are wrong. To get that three box deal on pizza you have to use that pizza coupon I cut out for you last week.

Ed - What pizza coupon? You never gave me a pizza coupon. You said that you were going to but you never did. If I know anything, I'm certain about that.

Margaret - Edward, I did give you that coupon. Without that coupon your "three pizza deal" doesn't exist. It will cost you $40 to buy three pizzas without that coupon.

Ed - Admit it Margaret, you lost my coupon. You did it on purpose because for some reason you would rather go out on Friday nights than stay at home, eat pizza and watch the Friday night fights on TV.

Margaret - For one thing, I didn't lose your coupon. You put it in your wallet. Another thing is I would like to go out at least once a year and lastly, I'd rather watch reruns of reruns of The Three Stooges than watch the fights. We need another television. If you weren't so tight we could actually get one in color. That piece of colored plastic that you taped to the TV screen just doesn't help at all. You know, if we actually got cable or a real antenna, we could get more than three channels.

Ed - I told you years ago when those cable people starting digging up the neighborhood for their cable lines that nobody would force me to buy cable. I showed them. Just think of all the money that I've saved over the last twenty years.

Margaret - You sure did. To get cable now, we would have to pick up the $300 cost for them to lay the new cable line in our yard. We might actually be able to see the shows we try to watch. I know that sometimes you can't even tell which fighter was which. You have to read it in the paper the next day to know who won.

Ed - I like my black and white set and I'm use to the jumping and the static. Where is your pioneering spirit? If we had a normal set – you wouldn't have anything to complain about.

 Margaret - I'd just like to be a typical American family - like having pizza on the TV tray in front of a color TV that is at least 21 inches. Most people think of the American Dream of owning your own home. Mine is having cable TV and a modern 21st century version of that thing called a TV set. We're still using the first one we bought in 1957.

Ed - I've told you before that if this one ever goes out, I'll buy a new one even though it will probably put us in the poor house.

Margaret - Edward, you spend more on tubes for that old set than a new TV would cost. Let me see your wallet.

Ed - Be careful, I have everything organized in there. There is a place for everything and everything is in its place in my wallet.

Margaret - Where did you hear that? Just going through your wallet shoots that theory to death and... would you look here. Just look, Rob's pizza special coupon, right in your wallet. What's more, here are those cents off coupons that you were supposed to use last week on triple coupon day at the Winn Dixie. How long has this wallet been organized?

Ed - Margaret, why don't I go order that pizza. What kind did you want? We have had such a stimulating discussion I forgot. You just let me know and I'll place that order right now. I'm picking it up to save a tip and the delivery fee.

Margaret - Edward, that gas guzzler that you drive most likely costs you more than having it delivered.

Ed - You act as if I'm a tightwad. I don't mind tipping. As a matter of fact I love giving a tip. I reminded the delivery kid to check his motor oil and that is an important tip. He must have really appreciated it because I could hear him mumbling to himself all the way back to his car. Another time I told the delivery boy that I appreciated his speedy service and for him to wait while I got the tip money. Boy was I wrong. He had a bad attitude. You should have seen him when I asked if he had change for a dollar.

**Ed comes home with the pizza and
– Margaret smells anchovies.**

Margaret - Ed, are you brain dead? Don't you recall the conversation that we had about anchovies? You promised that you wouldn't get anchovies! What's wrong with you? Oh, I bet I know! Are you wearing your hearing aid?

Ed - What Margaret, I can't hear you. My hearing aid is turned off.

Margaret - It doesn't work if you don't turn it on.

Ed - I 'm simply trying to make my batteries last longer. Do you know how expensive those things are? I only turn it on when we have company.

Margaret - Save money! Have you forgotten that your battery is rechargeable? Three thousand dollars for a hearing aid, you don't use and I can't even have cable TV.

Ed - We do too have a TV.

Margaret - That's not what I said. I said I can't have cable TV.

Ed - I'm glad that you don't want cable TV. I told you that it was way too expensive.

 Margaret - Here Ed let me turn that hearing aid on. CAN YOU HEAR ME NOW?

 Ed - Wow, Margaret you don't have to shout. Have a piece of pizza. I couldn't remember if you wanted extra anchovies or not, so I got extra on the side.

Margaret - You did what? Why I distinctly remember. Oh never mind. Give me a slice of that pizza. After living with you for fifty years, it's evident that you are not going to change, so I guess that I'm going to have to learn to eat them. Who knows? I may learn to like anchovies.

A Long Winter Night

Rodney Nall

Cast:

Ed is working late at the office when Margaret decides to keep him company.

Location:

It's Ed's office.

Ed- Well, I'm finished for the weekend. The next time I have to work nights at the office, I don't need company.

Margaret- But Ed, I just hate it when you go to work at night. You're all by yourself, and I'm all alone at home.

Ed – You've spent the entire evening asking questions. Where's the key to the powder room? Are you through yet? Can I help you? Do you have any more change for the vending machines?

Margaret – I'm sorry, I was just trying to keep you company.

ED –I can't wait to get home and get some sleep. Tomorrow's my pre-game Super Bowl Party.

Margaret – Everything's ready. The long neck beer is iced down and your favorite one-hundred wing special has been ordered. Just pick them up early tomorrow. I've got chips, salsa and the jalapeño casserole is simmering in the over.

Ed- Tomorrow's should be a day I'll never forget.

Margaret - Us girls are going to the spa and have complete makeovers.

Ed – I can't believe you would rather go to a spa than watch the game. There won't be any wings or jalapeño casserole leftover after the game.

Margaret – You guys have to have iron cast stomachs to eat all that stuff. The girls will have a nice salad and hot tea. We need the TV by twelve so we can catch the Home Shopping Channel's "Midnight Special".

Ed - I've been here for six hours, and I should have been through in two.   Let's head for the elevator. I want to go home, shower and hit the bed.

Margaret – At least you didn't get lonesome.

Ed – Lonesome was not the problem.

Margaret – Look how dark it is in the hallway. Let's hurry to the elevator. I'm scared, hungry, and thirsty and I want my **OWN** bathroom.

Ed - Here's the elevator. Let's get out of here.

Margaret- Now isn't this cozy. Did you get everything? Do you need some help holding your stuff?

Ed – My arms are full but I can manage just fine. Move over so I can get in the elevator and move your purse so the elevator door will close.

Margaret – I love this elevator! Look, it even has a wall mirror so you can check out your makeup.

Ed - Yeah that comes in handy every time I need to check on my mascara.

Margaret - This a very nice elevator and it runs so smooth. You can't even tell it's moving.

Ed – This is a high speed that will zip us down in no time at all.

Margaret –You can't even tell we're moving.

ED, WE'RE NOT MOVING! ...., WE'RE STUCK!!

Ed –Oh oh, everyone's left the building until Monday morning.

Margaret – Ed, I'm having trouble breathing?
Do something Ed, you're my husband, DO SOMETHING! I need to go to the bathroom.

Ed –It looks like we're going to be here for a while.
Do you still have that bottle of water in your purse?

Margaret - Ed I'm freezing! Let me have your coat. You've got enough fat that you won't freeze. I need your gloves too.

IT'S TWO AM AND ED AND MARGARET HAVE BEEN STUCK FOR FOUR HOURS IN THE ELEVATOR

ED – Margaret, you have worn me out and you have probably worn God out too. I can't see how you can keep all the promises you made. You promised to solve world hunger, cure cancer and become a nun. That's a lot, even in your lifetime.

 Margaret – Ed, I'm sorry for not being a better wife, I'll always be by your side and never complain, I-I…….. WAIT JUST A MINUTE! It's your fault we're locked in this cage. You dragged me down here last night. I could be home, not starving, not freezing to death, with no oxygen, and no bathroom!

Ed –Margaret, we'll be alright. It might just take a while.

Margaret - You did it on purpose, didn't you Ed? Do you love me? Are you having an affair?

Ed – I'm not having an affair.

Margaret – Ed, I can't breathe, you're using up all the oxygen. DON'T BREATHE SO MUCH!, WE"RE RUNNING OUT OF OXYGEN! HELP, HELP. HE'S TRYING TO KILL ME!! HELP!!

Ed – STOP IT! It was your idea to come with me tonight. We'll get out eventually. I am a little hungry. What are you eating? Are those breath mints? Give me some!

Margaret – They're all gone.

Ed - Why didn't you share?

Margaret – It's survival of the-the-the, well whatever. I was hungry! You don't want me to lose my girlish figure, do you Ed?

Ed – Never mind, I had a mini Snicker bar while you were taking a nap. I figured I needed all my strength to get us out of here. Here, you can lick the wrapper. I was saving it for later, but I'll share.

Margaret- Okay, I guess that makes us even.
I finished up the water bottle. It was hot, but I was thirsty.

Ed – Thanks a lot Margaret!

Margaret - I saw a movie where the man scaled the elevator wall, broke through the ceiling, pried open the door and saved his love. Do it, do it now! Show me you love me. Knock the door down Ed!

Ed – Margaret, stop it. I'm not a movie star. This is the real world. Just take another nap.

Margaret – I can't. I got a crick in my neck and I need to see my chiropractor! Where is a chiropractor when you need one?

Ed –When we first got on the elevator, which button did you push?

Margaret – Button, what button? Why would I push a button? I thought you pushed the button, after all it is the man's job.

Ed – Who's job? I had my hands full. Move over so I can push the parking garage button.

Margaret – Never you mind Ed, I'll do it.

Ed –I said I'll do it. If you do it, you'll tell everyone how you saved us. I'll never hear the end of it.

Margaret – Move over Ed. I said I'd do it. It's my right to save us.

Ed – SAVE US? You're the crazy person that stranded us.

Margaret – Wait a minute, let's do this the good ole' American way. Let's draw straws?

Ed- Have you got a straw? I thought not. We'll flip for it..if, I had a coin. You used all my change in the vending machine!

Margaret – You don't have a coin. I don't have a straw. What are we going to do?

Ed - Wait, have we gone crazy? We don't even know if we can get out. Push the button.
WOW….The elevator is moving. We're moving.
Look the door is opening, we're out of here!

Margaret – Just a minute Ed, before you get off the elevator you need to go back up to your office.

Ed – You are really losing it. There is nothing and I reiterate, nothing could make me go back to my office tonight. What could you possible need? Whatever it is, I'll get it Monday.

Margaret –I don't think so.
The keys to our house and your car are in the powder room, upstairs.

Part Time Job

By

Gerald Rodney Nall

Characters:

Margaret is helping her husband find a job.

Ed has his own idea of what job he can handle.

Location:

It's the home of Margaret and Ed.

Margaret - Ed, are you still looking at the help wanted section of the paper?

Ed -_If I keep looking, I'm confident that I will find my dream job. Did you realize that all jobs in the newspaper are listed in alphabetical order? They have listings for bartenders, custodians, and drivers.

Margaret -   Give it a rest Edward. You'll never find a job in today's economy.

 Ed - Margaret I just found a dream job. Let's see, it requires a commercial driver's license, and long– haul driver. Margaret, what does long haul mean? Of course I'd be there for the long haul. I've never quit a job until it was complete.

Margaret - Ed, long haul means driving a big rig across the country. My goodness, you have trouble just getting to Rick's Market and back home without getting lost. If you got that job, who would lay out your clothes for you each morning? You know you wouldn't eat right.

Ed - Come on Margaret, give me a little credit. In a few weeks I'd have that job down pat. Let me see, must be able to lift fifty pounds. Why'd I'd be able to work up to that in no time.

Margaret - Oh give me a break. The vacuum cleaner wears you down just plugging it in and five minutes of carrying a few groceries in from the car puts you down for a nap.

About the only thing you can lift regularly is that long neck beer bottle. Thirty years ago Doctor Brown, bless his soul, told you that a beer now and then would be good to help your appetite. Well now, there's nothing wrong with your appetite and you're still drinking.

Ed - Wow, here's an opportunity! They will allow me to become a business partner by investing in one of their eighteen wheeler trucks for only $85,000. It says that in only ten years it would be paid off and I'd be an owner operator.

Margaret - Ed, you're almost seventy and you don't have any money. Nobody's going to give you a loan and you certainly won't be working for ten more years.

Ed - It says right her that they are an equal opportunity employer.

Margaret - I would prefer that you open a massage parlor or sponsor a senior mud wrestling contest. At least we wouldn't have to mortgage the house to buy a truck.

Ed - Here it is! Part time plumber wanted. Experienced only! You know over the years I've done a lot of plumbing around our house so I'm experienced.

Margaret - How well do I know! If you remember, the last time you were going to repair a "small" leak, it ended up costing us more than $500. You can just forget about applying for that job. Ed, you need to look for some little ole' lady that needs her dog walked.

Ed - Margaret, Margaret, I found it. I found a job. Its inside, has flexible hours, and pays a little better than minimum wage, a dream job!

Margaret - Let me see that ad!

Ed - Margaret, it could be the start of a whole new career, better still, a whole new me. With a little luck I could make enough to start paying taxes again. Wow, Margaret, I can be somebody again.

Margaret -   The ad says; "Wanted, a mature person, preferably a retiree, to work part-time, flexible hours." Ed, did you read the entire ad? They want a "Greeter" down at the local store.

Ed - You're just jealous! You are afraid that I'll become the bread winner again and you couldn't stand that. I need extra money to add to my comic book collection. You realize that's going to help when the kids put us in the "Home." I'll just cash my classic comic book collection in and we can live on our own in the lap of luxury.

Margaret -   The comic book collection is only worth what someone is willing to pay for it. With our social security, your pension and the savings we don't have, we'll be lucky if we can find a dorm room with six beds and a television set to share with the other people living in the room.

Ed - I was thinking more like a private master bed room, a private bath, a big screen television, room service, a golf cart to run around the Country Club Estates and free movies. If they apply our senior citizen discounts, that would help, wouldn't it?

Margaret - You know that the kids said we could move in with them. You could do the yard work and clean the pool and I would have to do all the cooking. That would be a problem since they never like what I cook. They live on pizza, fries, and cheeseburgers. The grandkids would have all their friends over for parties and music, loud music. We would never have any quite time or be by ourselves.

Ed - Last summer I was mowed their yard with my riding lawn mower and someone called in and reported me for not wearing a shirt in public. I couldn't believe it when the sheriff's deputy showed up and threatened to give me a ticket for indecent exposure

Margaret -_ Oh Ed, it's just too much to think about moving in with the kids.

Ed - I'd have to forget about a vegetable garden in their neighborhood. I've never seen so many restrictions in a neighborhood.

Margaret - How about a paper route? They are always advertising for help. You could haul the papers in your wagon and get some exercise. But, remember, the neighborhood boy quit delivering when he realized that 5 AM comes every morning, 365 days a week.

Ed - Well, you just talked me out of the paper route. We had a terrible winter last year and a ton of rain this summer. If I had to drive my car due to bad weather with gasoline at $1.19 per gallon, I'd go in the hole each month.

Margaret - Ed, maybe it's just not meant for you to have a part-time job. I'd hate to see anything disrupt your daily schedule. You'd miss your two hour nap every afternoon and think about all the TV soap operas you would have to miss.

Ed - I do need my nap and I'd miss my soap operas.

Margaret - The neighbor ladies would miss you. Who else could they talk about every day? The ladies never know which Ed will come out each morning. There is the unshaven bum with holes in his pants, a crazy hat of the day and a worn out shirt. Then we have the suave, cool senior that dresses like he's going to church. Some of the neighbors think there are two men living here.

Ed - Margaret, it's just that I hear about people discovering themselves late in life. Colonel Sanders invented fried chicken with secret special spices. Grandma Moses learned to paint. Moses learned leadership in the bible. I just believe that life has more to offer for 'ole Ed Blakely.

Margaret - Now listen to me, Ed Blakely, we've had a good life. You helped raise a good family and you have always been a good provider. Together we put the kids through college. They got married and have never gotten into any serious trouble. We owe no bills, the house is paid for and we can buy the groceries we like and even eat out occasionally.

Ed - Well, Margaret, you made me feel mighty proud. I get down sometimes and feel I could have done better. I know one thing that I did right. That's when the preacher asked me if I took you for my wife and I said, "I do."

Margaret - Oh Edward, you are going to make me cry! The best is yet to come.

Spring Cleaning

By

Rodney Nall

Cast:

Ed, the husband, drives Margaret crazy.
Margaret, the wife, has her hands full.

Location:

It's Spring Cleaning as
Ed and Margaret sort things out.

Margaret - EDWARD, get up off that couch this minute. I know that you're not asleep. When you sleep, the entire neighborhood knows it. I get so embarrassed from your snoring. Get up! I can tell you're faking and I know why. Now open those baby blues and tell me what's going on.

Ed - What, what do you mean, "What's going on"? I was sound asleep. I was dreaming about winning the lottery. I was dreaming of spending it all on you. The first thing I was going to do was buy you a brand new fur coat. I've started a list of "dream items" just for you. I'm planning a cruise to Alaska. Then I'm…

Margaret - Why you big bag of wind, to think of you as a big spender is very funny. You never   buy me a valentine, birthday or anniversary gift. Yesterday, you bought a one dollar lottery ticket with odds one in thirty million, and you are already the world traveler. I can read you like a book. You're trying to change the subject, but it will not work this time! What did we agree to just this morning?

ED - I seemed to have forgotten. What was that, Margaret?

Margaret - Don't give me that what do you mean . You promised to clean out the garage and your office. You've been retired ten years and you haven't done a thing to that office, in

fact it's worse. You never throw anything away.
After all these years, it's taking over the house.

Ed - Now just hold on. I did pick out what I don't need and I put it out on the driveway for the trash collectors to haul off.

Margaret – Well, for once you're actually telling the truth. You did load up a lot of stuff. The only problem is that all that "stuff" you threw away was my stuff.
What about all you're bowling trophies,
those sales awards from forty years ago,
the moose you shot by accident while you were duck hunting and mounted it as a trophy?
You have two shelves of word puzzles, and
Hess trucks in the original boxes you've had for the past thirty years. You have exercise equipment, sacks of empty glass baby food containers, and piles of newspapers that you once saw an article in that you might like to look at later or like never.

Ed - Now Margaret, you specifically said to get rid of items I don't need. I didn't need any of your things, so I dumped them. Everything that's left in the garage is essential to my well being. For instance, all my monthly performance reviews from my forty years on the job. What if I need some of those as a reference when I apply for my "dream job"? All my old bosses have already passed away and those reports are all I have to prove what a great employee I was.

Margaret - You threw out my antiques.

Ed - What? You have got to be kidding. Those boxes of Tupper Ware have to be fifty years old.
Most are cracked and yellowed and there is so much of it.
What do you plan to do with so much Carnival Glass? The

peddle sewing machine was so covered in dust I couldn't tell what it was. The quilting frames are warped. There are plastic trash bags full of material remnants everywhere.
You have hundreds of copies of <u>Better Homes and Gardens</u> magazines. I'm exhausted, my back hurts, my hay fever is acting up from all that dust and I need a nap so I can watch TV tonight. The Gene Autry reruns start tonight. Turner Classic is going to run thirty-six hours of Gene Autry and Champ.

Margaret - You, you, you're awful. I just take a little space for myself. I ask for so little and you try your best to make me feel guilty. I haven't even mentioned all the computer towers you've collected and there are several computer key boards. You have dozens of boxes of floppy discs, unlabeled floppy discs. That is nothing compared to the forty years of National Geographic's with all those naked pictures. The number of cigar boxes that you've collected is unbelievable and I'll never know why you saved all those Prince Albert tins.
The cigarette machine you bought in the early seventy's that cost $382 is still in the box. You quit smoking cigarettes years ago and now you only occasionally have a rum soaked cigar.

Ed - See Margaret, it's all about your stuff.
Everything you mentioned of mine has real value.
The kids can probably send our grandkids to college when they sell our stuff after we're gone.
My solid gold safety razor alone has to be worth enough to make Fort Knox jealous.

Margaret – Now, I know you've lost all sense of reality. That "solid gold safety razor" that you are referring to is gold plated. The gold has worn off and you only paid a couple of bucks for it

in 1955.
Your visions of grandeur are slightly exaggerated.

Ed - Now wait just a second, I know what real gold feels like.
I've kept my "lucky gold penny" in my wallet for over forty
years. I've kept it shiny new and it continues to bring me good
luck.

Margaret - Now I know that you are loony as a goose.
That's not a gold penny, its copper.

Ed - Picky, picky, picky, that's what you are.
You're always just looking for something.
I'll make you a deal. I'll move all of the stuff back in the garage
and let's wait until next year to clean out the garage.

Margaret - Some things mean so much to me, I can't do
without them. Did you happen to see my wigs boxes from the
seventy's? I just might start wearing them again.

ED - I'd like to find my collection of barbed wire that I collected
as a kid. I'll mount them on redwood and people will stand in
line for them.

Margaret - Maybe we can sort through our boxes of dreams
and find a place for all of them.

Ed – Margaret, it's no wonder I married you, you are a smart
woman. You know, the kids are going to go crazy when they
see that we still have all our bunch of stuff.

Margaret - That's okay Ed, let them create their own dreams.
Their time will come.

October Surprise

Halloween comedy

By

Rodney Nall

Cast:

Margaret is mending Ed's Halloween costume.
Ed the husband just wants a new costume.

Location:

Margaret and Ed are at home and Margaret is mending Ed's
Halloween outfit before Ed goes out for the night.

Margaret - Ed stop wiggling or I'll never get your Halloween costume finished. I've never seen a grown man act like such a baby. You've already made me stick myself with these straight pins half a dozen times. I need to get through so I can watch "Today's Special" on the cable shopping program.

Ed - All I said was, "I'm going to Halloween Outlet Central to buy my Halloween outfit" and you had a fit. Everything is advertised at twenty-five percent off, today only. Halloween is one of the few pleasures that I have left in life and you're trying to take it away. I wanted to pick out my own costume for a change. But no, I have to use the costume I've used for the last twenty years. I'm sick of it. I just wanted to......

Margaret - Would you quit complaining? The Little Bo Beep outfit looks so cute on you.

Ed - Cute, what grown man wants to be cute for Halloween? I want to be "ELVIS". These bloomers keep falling down and I have to stop and pull them up. I keep tripping over then and spilling my pumpkin full of candy. Once I even lost a box of red hots and you know how I love them. I didn't get another box all night.

Margaret - What other grown man dresses up for Halloween? You embarrass me to death running around the neighborhood

99

"tricking and treating". I still can't believe the neighbors give you anything, a grown man out by himself without any kids with him. You leave our neighborhood and go into that new subdivision. It's a wonder they don't call the cops.

Ed - Did you know the Browns just give penny candy and then only a couple of pieces? Like it or not, I'm the envy of the neighborhood. There's not one kid that gets more candy than me.

Margaret - I wouldn't say envy, it's more like pity. The neighbors have pity for the old man and especially pity for the poor woman that has to live with him. The only salvation for me is the pleasure I get giving out candy to the cute little kids that come by, WITH THEIR PARENTS.

Ed - Well, if you would let me decorate the house for Halloween I would probably stay home and help you pass out treats.

Margaret - What do you mean decorate the house? You have the front yard and the front of the house looking like a spider web. The only thing I put my foot down about was putting a casket in the front yard.

Ed - That casket looked really neat. What about the hearse?

Margaret - Oh, when you brought that 1957 Cadillac. Storing a casket under the house was bad, but having an antique hearse parked in the driveway all year long was over the line.

Ed - Margaret, that time you actually broke my heart. That Cadillac only had 20,000 miles on it and the mortician told me it had never been driven over 35 miles per hour and was serviced regularly. I will never be able to buy a Cadillac and that was a dream automobile, not a scratch on it. I actually thought you would love it. We could have gone camping in it. We could have driven it across the country and not paid one motel bill. There was plenty of room to sleep in the back,

Margaret - I didn't want to sleep in a hearse. Our relatives would have had heart failure if we had driven up in that thing. It was so long you had to park on the street. I let you keep it for a couple of weeks, but when the neighbors started bringing in food and sending cards of condolences, it had to go. I've never been so embarrassed.

Ed - I don't know what you were so upset about. We had enough food to last a week. It stopped coming in when word got around that no one had actually passed on.

Margaret - Here, try this on. I've had to add so much material to your Little Bo Peep Outfit over the years that it's beginning to look a little shabby. I'm glad you only wear it in the dark.

Ed - Margaret, I just want to be Elvis. I always dreamed of being the "The King". No one else has to wear old costumes. Everybody else gets to be something different every year.

Margaret - EDWARD, stop it. You whine more than any kid we ever had. I give up, you will not let up until you get your way. Go to that Halloween shop and get yourself an Elvis outfit.

Ed - Oh Margaret, thank you, thank you, thank you! I will never complain about your cooking again, no matter how bad it taste. I'll vacuum without being told. The shrubs will never look shabby again. I'll shave every day. I'll never track mud in again.

Margaret – Go ahead and buy the Halloween candy. It'll save me a trip. Don't get those giant size or large four ounce bars, they're too expensive. Buy what's on sale, not what you like. I do not want to see a bag full of Snickers or Baby Ruth bars. I know you will eat them all yourself and then we'll have to go back to the store for more candy. Buy only wrapped candy. Parents don't like for their kids to get candy that's not wrapped.

Ed - Margaret, I didn't just fall off the turnip truck. I am an adult and can go shopping without being told every step to take. You never let me forget I got a little confused and got a couple of wrong items, a couple of times.

Margaret – Now, I'm a little confused. Do you recall buying that large bag of unwrapped beef jerky for Halloween two years ago? You're the only one that eats it. We couldn't give it out at Halloween and there are at least twenty pieces still in the pantry.

Ed – Margaret, I'm leaving, as soon as I find my hat.

Three hours later, Ed returns home

Ed - Margaret, I'm home. You are going to be so proud of me. I saved us a ton of money. You'll have plenty of goodies for all the little goblins that come to our house.

Margaret - Now, aren't you glad that we had that little talk before you went shopping?

Ed - Yes, Margaret, that was really helpful and I did bargain shop.

Margaret - Let me see what you have in the bag, or rather bags? How much did you buy?

Halloween is only one night. What is this, caramel popcorn? Ed, this is not individually wrapped. You have several bags. In fact you have twelve bags, large bags, very large bags of caramel popcorn. It's bulk caramel popcorn. Where was your head when I was talking to you before you went shopping?

Ed - Wait just a minute, you told me to buy what was on sale, and this was on sale. The man was marking it down since it was out of date. He said it still tasted pretty good even though it had gotten kind of sticky, but for this price, I couldn't go wrong. Besides that, it even looks like Halloween candy. It has that nice bright orange color. He said that if I would buy it all, he'd even help me carry it to the car. Something about getting it out of the store before his boss found out that it was left in the storage room.

Margaret - I can't give this out for Halloween. It is so sticky? This will be a terrible mess. Ed, did you taste this stuff? Which year did he say it went out of date?

Ed - Why do you always have to be so hard to please? Just look! I stick my hand in, grab a handful and just like Colonel Sanders, its finger licking good. I simply lick my fingers. You worry too much. It doesn't taste so bad. The caramel flavor covers up the old popcorn taste. I've burnt popcorn that tasted worse than this.

Margaret - Ed, we are not giving this mess for Halloween. I'll go to the store myself. My dad always told me, "If you want something done right, do it yourself." I'm taking this caramel popcorn back. I'll pick out the candy for Halloween.

Ed - Margaret, you need to give me another chance. I have found the secret to improving my mind. I've been doing crossword puzzles and word games. It's a surefire way to good mental health. Since I've been doing those word games, my brain has been energized, you know like the energized bunny. My mind is like a steel trap. Nothing gets by me. I forget nothing. I'm a new man. Do you remember that song called "I Am Woman". Well, I might write one called, "I Am Man". Yeah, Yeah!!!!

Margaret - I have to tell you Ed that sounds pretty impressive. You know I could be completely wrong. However, there is one thing, "Mr. Energized Bunny", that never forgets anything.

Where is your Elvis outfit?

Christmas Spirit or Holiday Blues

By

Rodney Nall

Cast:

The Announcer

Margaret

The house wife is getting ready for Christmas.

Ed

The husband doesn't get in any hurry and time slips away.

Clerk: 1

At the local handy man store

Clerk: 2

At a Lingerie Shop

Ed's neighbor:

Meets up with Ed shopping

Scene 1:

The scene opens at the home of Margaret and Ed.

Scene2:

Ed is finally shopping at the mall.

THE HOUSE SMELLS OF FRESH BAKED GOODS, TURKEY IN THE OVEN AND CIGAR SMOKE

Margaret – Ed, if you can pull yourself away from "The Gong Show", I need you to go to Garnett's Market. I need some eggs for the coconut crème pies that your aunt Lily loves. I also need some red ribbons, thin, not wide, some Christmas paper, extra wide scotch tape, double sticky side, cranberry sauce, jellied, not whole, a large can and.....

Ed – WHOOA! Have you got all that written down? Do you need it now? You know how I hate to miss the Gong Show.

Margaret – Ed, the Gong Shows are reruns.
Here I've written it all down for you.

Now get out of that recliner and hurry back.
Don't forget to use the coupons. This is double coupon day and
make sure to get the right size.
Make sure you buy the store brand for the items you don't
have coupons for.
Use the "rain check" receipt for the marshmallow crème. Do
not pay regular price.
I've written that in red ink on the side.
Stay away from the candy section. You don't need those
orange slices or chewy spice drops. The doctor said to watch
your sugar.
No more girly magazines either, I found yours hidden in the
family Bible.

Ed- I told you that I buy those magazines for the articles. I
didn't even know about those pictures until I got home. It did
have a very educational centerfold. I never knew that anyone
could get their body in that position. In fact, I may go back to
school to study the human body. IT'S A BEAUTIFUL THING!

Margaret - Just where did you put that centerfold? I know you
didn't throw it away.

Ed – I simply hung it above my workshop bench as inspiration.
When I start medical school, I...

Margaret – You're over sixty-five and you are not going to
medical school.

Ed – A man can dream can't he?

Margaret – It depends on what he's dreaming about. When
you get back I need you to vacuum the den and clean up your
bathroom. Heaven knows, you are the only one that uses that
bathroom and I don't want our company to think I don't keep a
clean house. Also, don't forget, you have to wrap the presents

you've bought for your relatives and….anyone else, that's really special to you. Heaven knows, you've had enough hints with Items circled in red and the ad section left out beside your prune juice every morning.

Ed – Presents, hints, suggestions………I—I---, oh sure! Everything is under control. Got to go! I'll see you later.

THREE HOURS LATER WITH ONE MORE STOP BEFORE HEADING HOME

Clerk – O.K. sir--- here we are in the drill section. Just how much money were you planning to spend on your wife's Christmas drill? I'm sure she will be so proud. We have some new sanders that would be very nice. You also mentioned the tool belt with all those screw drivers and pliers, assorted wrenches and…………Did I mention we have all our latex gallon paint on sale? You're a very lucky man to have such a practical wife.

Ed – I don't know. She is so hard to please. She always likes to be practical. I'll probably be back. I'll look around a little more.

ED STOPS AT A LINGERIE SHOP

Clerk - Yes, sir, may I help you. Everything is pretty well shopped over, but we have a few things that will spice up your life. Some nice choices are our "SEE THROUGH ID I BITTY SHEER" pajamas.

Ed – They're pretty nice, but how much are they?

Clerk – Today's Christmas Special, for all last minute shoppers is only, $88.95 plus tax.

Ed – What? Just one question, where's the rest of it?

Clerk – That is the rest of it sir!

Ed- But-t-t-t, Margaret would freeze to death in those. She just freezes in cool or cold weather. Do they come in flannel, wool or burlap?

Clerk – I'm afraid you are in the wrong shop. Since it's Christmas Eve we are closing for the night. You might try E-Z – Mart Outdoor Living. It's right down the street. I'm sure you'll find something down there that's just right for your wife. They sell long handle red underwear and wool bloomers.
Have a Merry Christmas sir.

LATER ED IS ON A DESERTED PARKING LOT TRYING TO WRAP HIS PRESENTS & A NEIGHBOR APPROACHES.

Neighbor- Why it's Ed. Hey Ed, what are you doing on the parking lot on Christmas Eve? I thought I was a late Christmas shopper, but you've got me beat.   What you doing with all that old wrapping paper on the hood of your car?

Ed- These are my Christmas presents. I've been wrapping for the last hour. I didn't realize how hard it is to wrap presents when the wind is blowing. There wasn't room in the car so I had to do it on the hood. Those clerks were going to charge me six bucks to wrap these. Besides, Margaret always says it's the thought that counts.

Neighbor- Well I'm surprised that you found anything this late on Christmas Eve. Say, did Margaret ever get a hold of you? She called the house about three hours ago and she sounded a little out of sorts. She said she had called the hospital and inquired if you had been in an accident and needed medical attention? If not, she said you were going to need some shortly.

Ed- What time is it? I knew it was dark outside, but you know how day light savings time messes everything up. By the way, do you like these?

Neighbor- What is it? What size is that and who did you buy it for?

Ed- I bought these for Margaret. It was the sexiest I could find. These bloomers look a little big, but Margaret likes her clothes a little loose. These bloomers are what hunters wear in sub-freezing weather, so I know Margaret will stay warm. They only had them in black and sizes 3X and up.
Every store was out of Christmas paper, but I got this great deal on Happy Birthday paper. It's got water stains on it, but as the clerk said, it's the thought that counts.

Neighbor- Is that all you bought Margaret?

Ed- No way, I got a great deal on ladies perfume. Margaret buys small little bitty bottles, but she will never believe I found it in a quart bottle. The clerk couldn't get the top off but she guaranteed it smells. She said that it's an acquired smell. It was the last bottle and they are not making this particular brand anymore.

Neighbor- Ed, they do not sell perfume by the quart. It's sold by the ounce. I'm sure Margaret will explain that to you later tonight. Ed, it might be better if you tell Margaret that you got lost. Otherwise, I think that you're a brave man.
If you need somewhere to sleep tonight, you know where I live. Merry Christmas Ed!

Ed gets home, his driveway is full and cars are parked up and down the block. It looks as if the guests have arrived.

Ed- I'm in trouble, AGAIN. The bathroom didn't get cleaned. The vacuuming wasn't done. The wrapping paper and tape are late as well as the groceries. Margaret is going to be livid with me. Where did the time go! No wonder Margaret does her shopping early. She starts her shopping for the next year with the after Christmas Sales. When will I ever learn? Let's see, what's my excuse?

 Did I get mugged?

Was I stuck in traffic?

The car wouldn't start!

Boy, nothing sounds very good and Margaret can tell when I'm lying. I might as well go on in and get it over with.

Oh well, there's always next year.

MERRY CHRISTMAS EVERYONE

Made in the USA
San Bernardino, CA
20 February 2015